Table of Contents

MW00903844

The Flight Locks, as seen from Lock 6, looking north toward Lake Ontario. (Linda Telega)

FRONT COVER - The FEDERAL ST. LAURENT departs Lock 4 downbound to Lake Ontario. CANADIAN PROVIDER (background) has just entered Lock 6 to begin its trip through the Flight Locks. The Seaway logo appears on the water tower at right. (Thies Bogner, MPA, Welland)
BACK COVER - The CANADIAN OLYMPIC and other members of the Upper Lakes Shipping fleet await spring break-up at Port Colborne. (Thies Bogner, MPA, Welland)

First edition 1992, updated 1996. Revised 1999. Copyright 1999, Skip Gillham and Don Revell. All rights reserved.
No part of this publication may be reproduced, stored in a retrieval system, or transmitted in any form without the written permission of the publisher.

Vanwell Publishing Limited acknowledges the financial support of the Government of Canada through the Book Publishing Industry Development Program for our publishing activities.

Photographs by Skip Gillham unless noted otherwise.

PRINTED IN CANADA

2

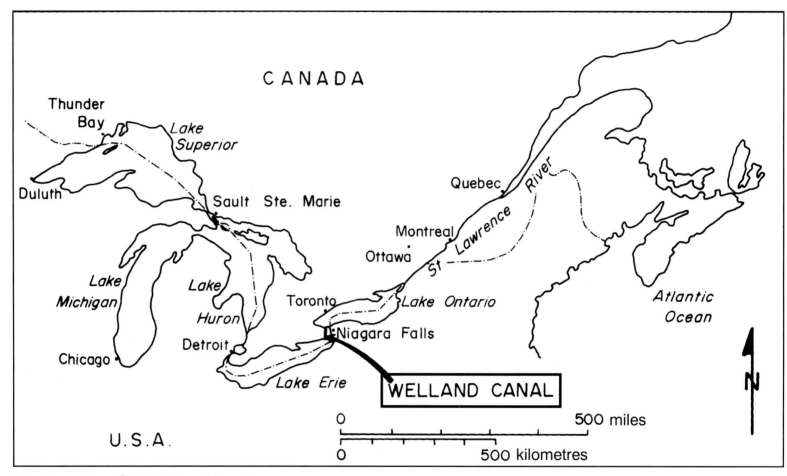

The Location of the Welland Canal

Foreword

Welcome to the Welland Canal — one of the greatest engineering accomplishments in Canada. It forms a key element in the St. Lawrence Seaway; a 4000 kilometre water route joining the industrial heartland of North America to the Atlantic ocean and world markets.

For more than 170 years, this canal and its predecessors have contributed to the economic and cultural development of the North American continent.

In 1994, the motor vessel PATERSON carried a record 29,016 metric tonnes of grain down the Welland Canal en route to the lower St. Lawrence. The canal, through its well-designed lock system, is also able to lift upbound vessels of a similar weight the approximately 99.1 metres (325 feet) required to cross the landform barrier presented by the Niagara Escarpment.

On a busy day twenty-four ships may traverse the Niagara Peninsula using the canal system. The average time required for a ship to travel between Lake Erie and Lake Ontario is twelve hours.

We hope this book will help you gain a deeper understanding and appreciation for this unique waterway.

Skip Gillham
Don Revell

About the Authors

Don Revell and Skip Gillham both hail from the Niagara Region and have always been fascinated by the Welland Canal. Skip has written a number of books about shipping and the canal and is a recognised authority on the subject. Don has a strong background in geography and outdoor education, and is the author of several textbooks. Both are retired from the Lincoln County Board of Education.

1 The History of the Welland Canal

Third Welland Canal circa 1885. A typical "Canaller" of the period in Lock 19 upbound (south) towards Thorold.
(Courtesy: St. Catharines Historical Museum N2215)

William Hamilton Merritt.
(Courtesy: St. Catharines Historical Museum)

PRE-CANAL ERA

Since the earliest times, the Great Lakes-St. Lawrence Waterway has provided travellers with an easy route deep into the interior of the North American continent.

Extending for approximately 4000 kilometres (2500 miles) from the beginning of Lake Superior in the west to tidewater in the east, at the mouth of the St. Lawrence, this waterway facilitated the early exploration and settlement of much of the central eastern portion of the continent.

As early as 1669, Adrien Jolliet, in his exploration of the New World to claim lands for France stood at the edge of Niagara Falls, in awe of this natural wonder. The normal route into the interior had been up the St. Lawrence River, north up the Ottawa River and then west down the French River to Georgian Bay.

On his return from Lake Superior Adrien Jolliet detoured from this route and proceeded southwards through Lake Huron to Lake Erie. He then paddled down the Niagara River, portaging around Niagara Falls, to Lake Ontario. By this detour, he opened a new route to the interior and subsequently eliminated many small time-consuming portages.

Nevertheless, until 1829 the waterfalls and rapids created by the Niagara Escarpment presented a formidable barrier to any movement of goods and people by water.

In 1829, this problem was finally overcome with the completion of the First Welland Canal, the brainchild of William Hamilton Merritt, an enterprising businessman of the Province of Upper Canada.

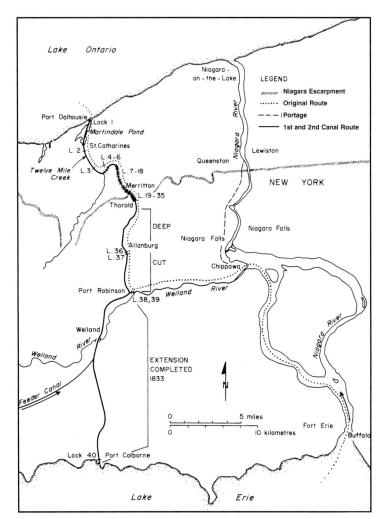

The First and Second Welland Canal

THE FIRST WELLAND CANAL

William Hamilton Merritt was born in 1793 in Bedford, New York. His parents, being loyal to the British Crown, left the newly formed United States to build a new home in territory that was still under British control - Canada.

Those that left the United States at that time to establish themselves in Canada have been called the United Empire Loyalists, and many came to settle in the Niagara Peninsula. Merritt's father received a grant of land from the Crown on the Twelve Mile Creek, a waterway that was to attain considerable significance in later years, when the route of the First Welland Canal was surveyed.

Merritt became a successful mill owner and merchant. He speculated that a substantial profit could be realized from toll fees if a navigable route across the Niagara Peninsula from Lake Ontario to Lake Erie could be constructed. From this idea, the Welland Canal Company was formed by an act of legislation, and construction was started in 1824. Both private funds and government grants were used to finance this venture.

This first canal utilized many of the existing landform features. The entrance to the northern part of the canal from Lake Ontario was through a large protected bay, presently called Martindale Pond. The village of Port Dalhousie was established on the northwest shore of the bay.

After traversing this bay, the route of the first canal followed the Twelve Mile Creek upstream to a point where a series of locks had to be constructed to take the ships up across the escarpment. A channel (the Deep Cut) was then cut from the top of the escarpment southwards to Chippawa Creek (presently the Welland River).

Ships could then move from Lake Ontario through Martindale Pond, upstream via the Twelve Mile Creek, across the Niagara Escarpment, through the Deep Cut to Chippawa Creek, down Chippawa Creek to the Niagara River, some 4 kilometres (2.5 miles) above the falls. The boats would then travel up the Niagara River to Lake Erie.

The first ships to cross the Peninsula using this new waterway did so in November 1829, some five years after the start of construction.

Vessels passing from Lake Erie down the Niagara River found they had considerable difficulty travelling upstream on the Chippawa Creek. Ships heading to Lake Erie had the same difficulty moving against the current in the Niagara River.

As a result, plans were made to eliminate these navigational problems and at the same time increase traffic capacity by extending the channel southwards from Port Robinson to Lake Erie (Port Colborne). This extension was completed in 1833 and the First Welland Canal was heralded as one of the most spectacular engineering feats in North America.

In order to ensure an adequate volume of water to float the vessels traversing the canal, a feeder canal was constructed to bring water from the Grand River at Port Maitland and Dunnville, farther west on Lake Erie. This feeder canal, although having a depth of only 1.2 metres (4 feet), was also used by smaller vessels as a subsidiary route through the Welland Canal.

The first canal was 44.3 kilometres (27.5 miles) long and had 40 wooden locks. The smallest of these locks was 33.5 metres (110 feet) long, 6.7 metres (22 feet) wide and could accommodate ships with a draft of almost 2.4 metres (8 feet).

Boats with cargoes of up to 145 tonnes (160 tons) were able to use this new canal.

In 1841 the Government of Upper Canada purchased the privately held stock and the Welland Canal was made one of Canada's first "Crown Corporations".

THE SECOND WELLAND CANAL

After purchasing all private holdings in the Welland Canal Company, the Province of Upper Canada embarked on an extensive scheme between 1842 and 1850 to improve the existing canal.

There was no significant change in the route taken by this second canal. Construction was parallel and adjacent to the original canal. The locks were made larger and were constructed of stone quarried from the Niagara Escarpment. The original 40 locks were replaced by 27 locks that would allow ships up to 42.7 m (140 feet) in length carrying cargoes of up to 454 tonnes (500 tons). These new locks were 45.7 m (150 feet) by 8 m (26.5 feet) and were constructed to a depth of 3 m (10 feet). Fewer locks were required by increasing the lift of each one.

Because the City of St. Catharines was rapidly becoming the major urban centre in the northern part of the Niagara Peninsula, special provision was made in construction of the locks to allow larger vessels of up to 54.8 m (180 feet) to travel upstream from Lake Ontario to that city.

The water flowing from these early canals was used to power the various grist mills located along their length. The increased flow resulting from the construction of the Second Canal created an additional source of power that attracted many other industries.

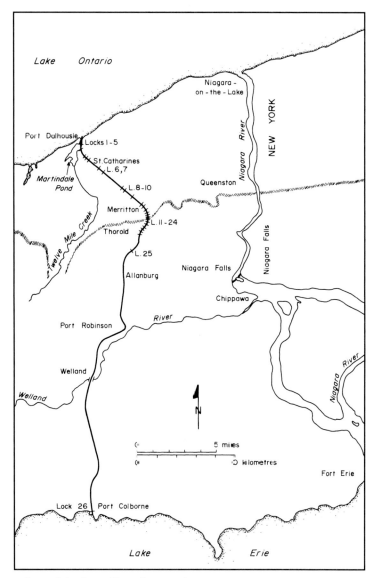

The Third Welland Canal

THE THIRD WELLAND CANAL

By 1870, steam was replacing wind as the primary source of power for the ships on the Great Lakes. At the same time, an increased volume of traffic was creating problems for the Welland Canal.

In 1871, a commission was established to suggest solutions to these traffic problems. The main suggestion resulting from this investigation was that the existing Welland Canal be modernized to conform to the lock size found in the St. Lawrence River between Lake Ontario and Montreal. As a result, 26 cut stone locks, 82.3 m (270 feet) long, 13.7 m (45 feet) wide with a 4.3 m (14 foot) depth were completed in 1887.

The southern two-thirds of the route remained essentially the same but a new and more direct route was constructed from the Niagara Escarpment to Port Dalhousie.

At this time, both the grain export trade and the steel industry were making great demands on the Welland Canal. Almost immediately after the completion of this Third Welland Canal, surveys were started in order to plan for another larger canal. By 1912, a new canal, the fourth, had been planned and the purchase of the necessary land was started. This fourth canal is the one presently in use by vessels travelling between Lake Ontario and Lake Erie.

THE WELLAND CANAL OF TODAY

Construction began on the present canal, the Fourth Welland Canal, in 1913 with the plan to reroute the northern section and build larger locks with a greater lift.

The 40 locks of the original canal were replaced by 8 new locks. The 7 locks in the northern portion are 261.8 metres (859 feet) long, 24.4 metres (80 feet) wide and have an average lift of 14.2 metres (46.5 feet). Ships, however, are not allowed to use the canal if they are longer than 224.5 metres (736.5 feet) or wider than 23.1 metres (75.8 feet), or with a draft in excess of 8.2 metres (27 feet). The water depth of the locks is 9.1 metres (30 feet) when completely filled. This requires about 95.5 million litres (21 million gallons), and it takes between 9 and 15 minutes to fill one of the locks.

The route of the northern section of the Third Canal had been abandoned for a more direct route to Lake Ontario. This part of the canal was straightened to an almost direct north-south line following the water-course of the Ten Mile Creek. At the northern terminus of the Fourth Canal an artificial harbour, Port Weller, had to be created by constructing two embankments extending 2.4 kilometres (1.5 miles) into Lake Ontario.

This Fourth Welland Canal was officially opened on August 6, 1932 when the LEMOYNE, the largest freighter on the Great Lakes, steamed into the upper end of the twinned flight locks.

There was one major modification yet to be made to this canal. The channel in the vicinity of the City of Welland was narrow and twisting. In addition, by bisecting the City of Welland, the canal created major traffic disruptions. In order to overcome these problems, the channel was straightened and enlarged between Port Robinson

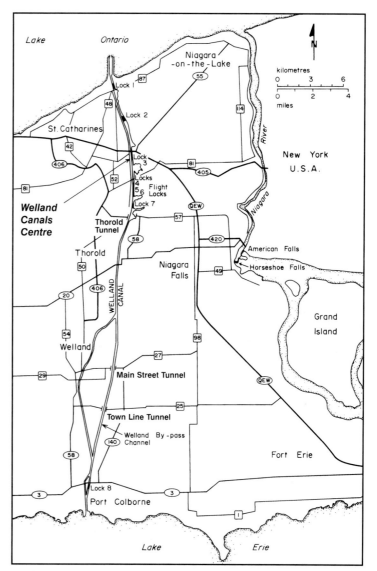

The Welland Canal of Today

The small steamer JAMES STEWART is shown in Lock 1 at Port Dalhousie, October 17, 1959. The lock remained in use for another decade. (Jay N. Bascom)

limit the mast height of ships to 35.6 metres (117 feet) above water level.

At almost any time during the navigational season, long lines of traffic may be seen at many of the bridges with motorists "patiently" awaiting the passage of some vessel.

For years a major tie-up of traffic would occur where the QEW crossed the Welland Canal at the Homer Bridge in St. Catharines. On October 18, 1963 the Garden City Skyway was officially opened to carry the QEW over the canal, creating a high-speed, controlled-access link between the New York Thruway and the densely populated areas of southern Ontario. The Garden City Skyway is 5.6 kilometres (3.5 miles) long and provides for six lanes of traffic. Engineers have also designed and constructed three tunnels under the canal to eliminate traffic problems.

THE LOCKS

Although there is a difference of 99.4 metres (326 feet) in elevation between Lake Ontario and Lake Erie, most of this change occurs in the northern section of the canal. Within 11.2 kilometres (7 miles), seven locks change the water level approximately 99.1 metres (325 feet).

In the southern section, the seventeen miles between Lock 7 and Lock 8 consist of a man-made channel crossing relatively flat land. Lock 8 at the Lake Erie end is a shallow lift lock, in place primarily to control the water intake into the canal.

The locks of the Welland Canal provide half of the lift to be encountered in the 4000-kilometre (2500-mile) waterway extending from the Atlantic to the head of Lake Superior.

and the City of Port Colborne. This "realignment" was completed in 1973.

As the Welland Canal crosses the Niagara Peninsula from north to south, major problems are created for the predominantly east-west highway and rail traffic. In all, there are ten railway and highway bridges crossing the canal. Three of the highway bridges have a vertical clearance for ships of 36.6 metres (120 feet). Regulations

Engineers have designed the locks so that gravity provides most of the force required to empty and fill these essentially watertight chambers.

A lock consists of a walled section of the canal closed off at either end by a gate. These gates are made up of two separate doors that close in a v-shape, pointing upstream. This has been engineered so that the downstream push of the water forces these doors tightly shut. There is a filling valve at one end and an emptying valve at the other (see page 14).

In order for a ship to descend through a lock, the vessel enters the lock through the upstream gate with the downstream gate closed (Figure A). Once it is in the lock, the upstream gate is closed, the ship is secured to bollards atop the lock wall, and then the emptying valve is opened (Figure B).

The canal traffic controllers try to regulate the movement of ships so that there is a vessel travelling upstream waiting to enter this now empty lock. The reverse process takes place after this up-bound ship enters the lock and it fills with water.

Although the filling (or emptying) of a lock takes approximately ten minutes, additional time is required for the ship to manoeuver in and out of the lock and tie up to the bollards. The average time required for the entire process, entering, changing elevation, and leaving the lock is thirty-three minutes.

Locks 4, 5 and 6 make up the famous Flight Locks. The steepness of the escarpment at this point has made necessary the construction of three continuous locks with no open channel between them. In addition these three locks have been twinned so that all three have both up-bound (west side) and down-bound (east side) chambers.

THE ST. LAWRENCE SEAWAY MANAGEMENT CORPORATION

A new group took over from the St. Lawrence Seaway Authority which had been established by the Canadian Federal government in December 1951 to construct, maintain and operate the seaway.

The new St. Lawrence Seaway Management Corporation took over the operation of a 3700-kilometre (2300-mile) portion of the Seaway on October 2, 1998. Only the area of the two American locks near Massena, NY, is not included. This section remains under the jurisdiction of the US St. Lawrence Seaway Development Corporation.

Nine companies are partners in the non-profit organization that will run the waterway. Representatives from each of the federal, Ontario and Quebec governments will also have a member on the board.

Lockage tolls are calculated on the size of the ship, weight and type of cargo, plus a flat fee for each lock. Pleasure craft are charged $10.00Cdn per lock.

12

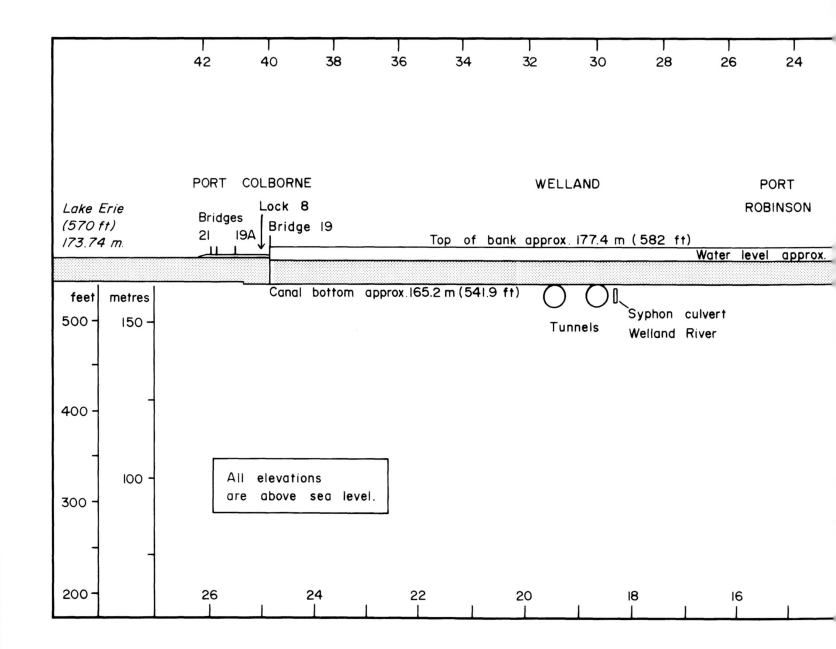

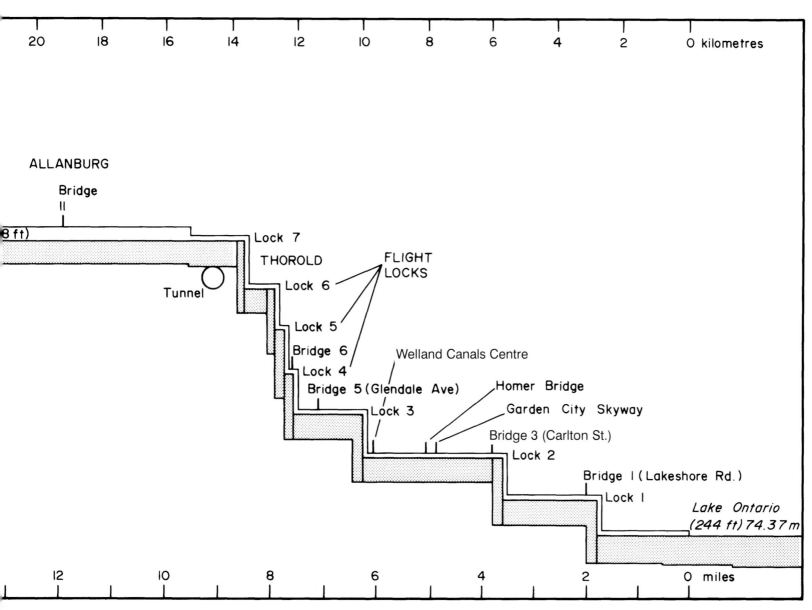

Cross Section of the Welland Canal

HOW THE LOCKS WORK - DOWN BOUND ROUTE

PROFILE VIEW

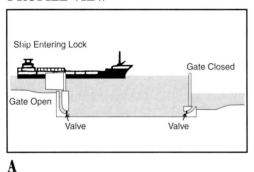

A

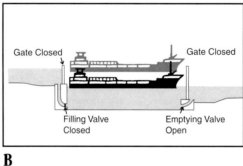

B

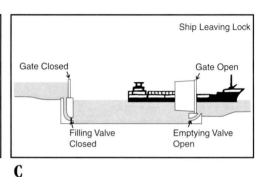

C

PLAN VIEW

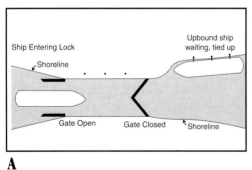

A

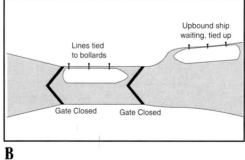

B

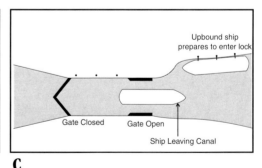

C

CANADIAN PROGRESS, a typical modern self-unloader, is inbound at the Port Weller piers.

BULK CARGO CARRIERS

ATLANTIC HURON, entering Lock 3, June 1, 1999.

The cheapest and most efficient method of transporting large volumes of bulk cargoes over long distance is by ship. On the Great Lakes commodities such as iron ore, coal, stone, grain and road salt are the most common payloads. There are also lesser amounts of sand, gypsum, coke, slag, potash, cement clinker, millscale and bentonite being transported.

These materials are carried in two types of ships, self-unloaders and straight-deck bulk carriers. The most common, the self-unloaders, are not dependent on costly shore-based equipment and personnel.

The interior cargo holds are modified to allow for a rapid discharge that often reaches 6000 tons per hour. The extra speed, shorter turnaround time and thus increased trips per season more than compensate for the slightly reduced carrying capacity and the cost of additional personnel on board to maintain and operate the equipment.

The cargo boom, stored on deck, can be swung over the side to deposit the various materials up to 76.2 metres (250 feet) from the ship.

Self-unloaders travelling through the Welland Canal may be carrying coal from Lake Erie to the steel mills in Hamilton, to Ontario Hydro's steam generating plant at Mississauga, or to the Gulf of St. Lawrence for trans-shipment overseas. Iron ore pellets from Lake Superior may be bound for Hamilton if downbound. Ships upbound with ore come from the St. Lawrence River for ports on Lake Erie, the Detroit River or Lake Michigan. Salt, stone and sand are in demand at many locations. Now several grain storage elevators have special hoppers to receive cargoes from self-unloaders.

The two newest types of self-unloaders feature a hopper system in the hold or operate with a single cargo hold and a reclaimer. The hopper type has a three-tunnel belt system. The cargo is fed by gravity through gates which control the unloading rate. Several cargoes can be handled in this system at the same time. A reclaimer type of self-unloader has a single cargo hold and therefore can haul only one type of cargo per trip.

The straight deck bulk carriers, once the backbone of the Great Lakes fleet, are in decline. They were built with an eye on efficiency but they have been surpassed by the self-unloaders.

In the early years of the Seaway almost every new bulk carrier had a new technique to increase carrying capacity.

When vessels switched from steam to diesel power they required a smaller engine room and thus provided for more cargo space. Lighter aluminum and plastic components reduced the weight of the ship itself and allowed for greater loads.

The ship's size was limited by the locks, and most were 222.5 or 224.5 metres (730 or 736.5 feet long). The PATERSON of 1985, the last new straight deck bulk carrier, can carry over 29,000 tonnes of wheat. This is enough to make three loaves of bread for every man, woman and child in Canada!

Grain and iron dominate the cargo logs of these Welland Canal giants. The grain usually is headed to the St. Lawrence for shipment overseas. The ore comes from ports on the St. Lawrence to steel mills on Lake Michigan. These ships may also carry coal, cement clinker and petroleum coke. A few smaller bulkers survive, and they also handle clay, pitch, fluorspar, salt and pig iron.

TANKERS

A great variety of liquid cargoes are carried by Great Lakes tankers. Most are equipped so they can handle numerous grades of petroleum products at one time without any fear of these products being mixed. Soon all tankers must have double hulls to minimize the chance of spills in the event of groundings or collisions.

Gasoline, both regular and unleaded, diesel fuel, stove and furnace oil, kerosene, aviation fuel, lube oil, bunker, varsol, benzene and naphtha as well as crude could be in transit in Great Lakes tankers.

They also handle chemicals such as calcium chloride and caustic soda. The Welland Canal tankers usually load petroleum products from the refineries at Sarnia, Bronte and Clarkson but others come up from St. Lawrence

AMELIA DESGAGNES, below Lock 2 on December 1, 1997.

The tanker ALGOSAR was built at Port Weller Dry Docks in 1974. (Roger Chapman)

STEPHEN B. ROMAN, inbound below Lock 1 on October 30, 1997, handles bulk cement.

The Panamanian-flag freighter HELENA OLDENDORFF, shown above Lock 1, April 25, 1998, has been a regular canal trader.

ports. Some tankers have duties in the Atlantic Provinces and they even travel to the Arctic to resupply the various outposts and bases during the limited northern navigation season.

CEMENT CARRIERS

The transportation of refined cement requires specialized equipment. The cement is so fine in texture that it must be loaded and unloaded through airtight pipes. Many of the current cement carriers have been converted for this work after years in other duties. It is not a coincidence that most of these ships are painted grey!

We continue to see both American and Canadian cement carriers travel through the Welland Canal. The American ships are more at home on the upper four Great Lakes but some, such as ALPENA and J.A.W. IGLEHART venture to Lake Ontario to load at Bath for US destinations.

ENGLISH RIVER and STEPHEN B. ROMAN are the principal powered Canadian haulers. Both are former package freighters that have been rebuilt. Although their routes are mainly on Lake Ontario, to Toronto, Oswego and Rochester, they also trade on the upper lakes.

In recent years St. Mary's Cement has employed barges for the run up the lakes from Lake Ontario ports. These vessels have their own pusher tugs.

DEEP SEA VISITORS

Deep sea ships call on the Great Lakes with cargoes from all over the world. The completion of the St. Lawrence Seaway in 1959 permitted much larger ocean freighters to trade on the freshwater lakes.

Prior to 1959, vessels using the locks between Lake Ontario and the St. Lawrence at Montreal could not exceed 79.55 metres (261 feet) in overall length.

The ocean ships hail from many locations. Some represent the interests of their nations while others fly "flags of convenience". In the latter category ship registry costs in certain countries worldwide are less than in the ship's own country.

Incoming cargoes vary and can include all types of manufactured goods. Steel is perhaps the most popular inbound payload but bulk quantities of special sand, ore or bauxite may be aboard.

Grain remains the dominant overseas shipment. This includes wheat, oats, barley, flax, soya beans, corn, canola, sunflower seeds, pinto beans, yellow peas and sugar beet pellets. In addition coal, potash, petroleum coke and scrap steel are handled.

Deep sea tankers leaving the lakes often carry chemicals such as liquid latex. On other occasions they haul vegetable oils such as linseed made from flax or inedible animal fats (tallow) and edible lard.

Container traffic has not had a big impact on the lakes. Specialized equipment for loading and unloading containers has been centralized on the east coast and St. Lawrence and the containers come further inland by road or rail.

Freight may travel on pallets, with some use of containers, or roll-on/roll-off carriers that have bow or stern doors to provide access to the cargo areas.

Project cargoes for developing countries, military hardware for an ally, farm machinery, or heavy lift items all travel down the Welland Canal for ports around the world.

The deep sea visitor GOVIKEN was flying the flag of Bahamas in 1997. (Dave Kohl)

HMCS SHAWINIGAN, a coastal defence vessel built in 1996, is among the Canadian naval vessels to pay courtesy visits to the Great Lakes.

The tug JAMES E. MCGRATH assists CANADIAN LEADER out of Port Weller Dry Docks on September 18, 1998.

The passenger vessel EMPIRE SANDY, shown under sail at Nassau on January 8, 1998 during winter work at the Bahamas, offers occasional charters through the Welland Canal, but only under engine power. (Al Mann)

Incoming freight cargoes span the imagination too. They include binder twine, jute, rubber, liquor, furniture, automotive parts, biscuits, garden tools and fruit juice concentrate.

The payloads travel in a variety of ships, large, medium and small. They come through the Welland Canal each year to serve ports all over the Great Lakes. When they depart they could be destined for any part of the world.

MISCELLANEOUS VESSELS

There are many types of craft using the Welland Canal, with a large variety of size and function.

Tugs, the workhorses of the waterfront, have many responsibilities. In the canal they may be travelling along to work on other parts of the lakes or they may be hauling barges or dredging equipment. Sometimes they provide power for freighters with mechanical problems. Above Lock 1 the JAMES E. MCGRATH assists big ships in and out of the Port Weller Dry Docks.

Barges are ships with no power source of their own. Some were once self-powered freighters, but for cost-saving reasons they are now propelled by tugs. Other barges may carry specialized equipment. Many are tank barges hauling liquid cargo.

Both the American and Canadian Coast Guard vessels provide icebreaking service in spring, late fall and early winter. These ships also place and remove navigational marker buoys in the shipping channels, perform search and rescue operations and environmental protection functions.

Passenger cruise ships are making a return to the Great Lakes but there is no regular tourist service through the Welland Canal. Several times a year Niagara College of Welland charters the EMPIRE SANDY for voyages through the canal and these are usually quickly sold out. Efforts to provide daily commuter service between the Niagara region and Toronto have been attempted using diverse craft such as hydrofoils, hovercraft, cruise ships and, recently a high-speed catamaran. These operations require more patronage to remain viable, however, and most have quickly been discontinued.

Pleasure craft, large and small, are regular users of the ship canal during the warmer weather. Private boat owners spend their holidays or retirement years travelling the lakes and there are many fine marinas above and below the Welland Canal. The number and quality of such facilities has grown at a rate reflecting the popularity of private cruising.

Naval vessels always draw a crowd during their canal transits. Large deep-sea ships of war make courtesy calls around the lakes in the summer and prove to be popular attractions. Some have been preserved as museums at lake ports such as Toronto which has the HMCS HAIDA, and Buffalo which has the USS SULLIVANS and USS LITTLE ROCK.

Smaller naval craft, built on the lakes for Canadian, American or foreign governments must use the Welland Canal to reach the sea.

Dredges used to maintain depths in harbours and channels may appear from time to time. Some are barges but some may be self-propelled.

CUYAHOGA, at Lock 7 on August 29, 1998, often carries salt on trips through the canal.

PATERSON, below Lock 8 on August 25, 1990, holds the tonnage record for grain through the Welland Canal.

3 Canadian Fleets of the Welland Canal

LOUIS R. DESMARAIS underway in 1997. (Dave Kohl)

CANADIAN FLEETS

Algoma Central Marine is the oldest and largest of the Canadian Great Lakes shipping lines and dates from 1899. They maintain a versatile fleet of self-unloaders, straight deck bulk carriers and, as of 1998, petroleum and chemical tankers.

Canada Steamship Lines specializes in self-unloader trades on both Great Lakes and deep sea routes. This firm was once the largest on the lakes. It was created in 1913 with the merger of a number of smaller operations.

Desgagnes Transport began with small wooden-hulled ships on the St. Lawrence. Their vessels have called on ports of the Great Lakes since the early years of the Seaway. These small vessels handle specialized bulk cargoes and they have now added two tankers.

Fednav is a Canadian company sailing the oceans of the world. Their red-hulled ships are common throughout the Seaway system and carry foreign registration. They usually bring steel inbound and depart with grain.

Lower Lakes Towing Ltd. began with tugs and barges but expanded in 1995 with the acquisition of the handy-sized self-unloader CUYAHOGA. This ship often visits the Welland Canal with salt, stone or grain.

McKeil Marine is based at Hamilton. They maintain a fleet of tugs and barges and are involved in a variety of trades and projects. Some of their tugs are regular canal travellers pushing liquid cargo barges.

P&H Shipping is the marine arm of Parrish and Heimbecker, noted grain merchants. They established their fleet in 1982 with the dissolution of the Soo River Company. The P&H ships serve mainly in the grain trade but also handle some iron ore.

N.M. Paterson & Sons Ltd. is a family operation with roots in the early part of this century. Most of their ship names end in the suffix "doc" which stands for Dominion of Canada.

Purvis Marine is based in Sault Ste. Marie and operates a small crane ship, the YANKCANUCK, as well as a number of tugs and barges.

Rigel Shipping Inc. has a fleet of tankers that serve Great Lakes ports as well as those on the St. Lawrence and in the Maritime provinces.

St. Mary's Cement has tug/barge combinations travelling the canal in the cement trade.

The Upper Lakes Shipping Group began during the Depression when other lake operators were going out of business. They grew to become a major force in lakes navigation, operating bulk carriers and self-unloaders. They are partners in Port Weller Dry Docks, a shipbuilding and repair facility above Lock 1 of the Welland Canal, and with Algoma Central Marine in Seaway Self-Unloaders and Seaway Bulk Carriers.

4 Canal Maintenance

The sides of Lock 4 East are being refinished as part of annual maintenance. This work is done in the winter months when the ships are idle and the locks can be drained. (Thies Bogner, MPA, Welland)

CANAL MAINTENANCE

Keeping the Welland Canal in operating condition requires constant maintenance. Preventive maintenance, repairs and long-term improvements take place all year round.

The system is usually shut down from January 1 until the last week in March. The locks are drained, as is much of the waterway between Lock 7 and Lock 1. If ships are berthed at Port Weller Dry Docks for winter work, the water level is only partly lowered between Locks 1 and 2. The Seaway uses their own staff plus sub-contractors to upgrade and repair the waterway during the winter months. Regular maintenance tasks include inspection of lock and bridge machinery, inspection of bridge structures, repairs to concrete both in the locks and along the tie-up walls, replacement of operating cables and rehabilitation of the bollards.

Recent improvements to the overall canal have been numerous. In 1973 the Welland By-Pass was opened between Port Robinson and Port Colborne. It eliminated the narrow channel, bends and bridges that dominated the earlier canal section.

Then, in 1980, the Guard Gate at Thorold was removed to speed navigation. A year later the tie-up wall on the east side above Lock 7 was extended.

Each winter, repair and maintenance projects are carried out at various points along the canal and in the locks.

Keeping the ships running smoothly, the equipment functioning and the structures sound is a large job but it is one that has been handled well in operating this vital link in the Canadian inland transportation system.

PROBLEMS IN MAINTENANCE

It is no easy task to keep a waterway like the Welland Canal operating smoothly and efficiently. Large ships moving through confined channels in a variety of weather conditions can tax any system. Although a few incidents over the years have drawn attention to the waterway these problems are most unusual.

Yet, in the over sixty-five-year history of the modern Welland Canal there have been accidents with serious consequences.

One of the most dramatic occurred on August 25, 1974 when the downbound freighter STEELTON hit the mid-section of Bridge 12 at Port Robinson, knocking both towers and the centre span into the water. All vessel traffic was plugged until September 9. The bridge was never rebuilt and today the village of Port Robinson remains divided.

On October 14, 1985 part of the wall in Lock 7 collapsed out. A large section of concrete caught the Liberian freighter FURIA as she was about to leave the lock. Repairs continued around the clock until the system reopened on November 7. This led the Canadian Federal Government to create a seven-year, $175 million program to refurbish the canal.

Other delays occur when a ship loses power due to engine failure and has to drop its anchor to stop its progress.

Sometimes a ship advances too far into a lock and hits the ship arrester cable. These structures have always prevented vessels from crashing through the lock gates but occasionally the device has been damaged sufficiently to hold up traffic.

LEADALE sank at Thorold after punching a hole in her stern.

Construction along the canal.

It is amazing that more collisions have not occurred, considering the number of possibilities that exist on a daily basis!

Among the casualties has been the former pilot boat QU'APPELLE which sank off the Port Weller piers. It had just taken a pilot out to an inbound foreign ship and struck the freighter's propeller while pulling away. It went down quickly but there was no loss of life. The QU'APPELLE was later refloated.

The mighty LEMOYNE, one of the best-known of all Canadian lake ships, brushed the stern of MARTIAN and then hit the Main Street bridge in Welland on June 29, 1966. It also demolished a barge and workboat en route, but fortunately there was no greater damage.

A few months later, on October 14, STONEFAX sank between Port Robinson and Allanburg after a collision with the deep sea trader ARTHUR STOVE. STONEFAX was secured and traffic resumed as the salvage effort proceeded successfully.

On December 7, 1982 the LEADALE backed from the dock at Thorold and hit a concrete dolphin, punching a hole in the stern. The vessel sank in twenty minutes but all of the crew were rescued. The hull was given a temporary patch, refloated, and towed to Port Colborne where it was scrapped.

It is a credit to the Seaway that there have not been more problems with navigation on the canal. A carefully planned system of traffic control, monitored via television in the Glendale Avenue headquarters, has the huge ships passing in optimum positions. When weather conditions become dangerous the waterway shuts down.

A crew of linesmen, lockmasters, draftsmen, bridge masters, electricians, carpenters, machinists, gardeners, mechanics, painters, riggers, welders, truck drivers, equipment maintenance men, all work behind the scenes to eliminate potential problems, clear up those that occasionally occur and keep the system running smoothly.

Two pleasure craft head upbound while the J.W. MCGIFFIN enters Lock 3. The Garden City Skyway can be seen in the background.
(Thies Bogner, MPA, Welland)

The Welland Canal has had a tremendous economic impact on the surrounding communities. Some aspects are obvious, others less so.

Ships move about the Great Lakes loading and unloading at different ports. For many, one consistent element in their travels is the Welland Canal and most Canadian lakers pass upbound or downbound on a regular basis. As a result many sailors locate their families in the Port Colborne, Welland and St. Catharines area so that they can visit them more often.

Many ship owners have either their headquarters or branch offices in the Welland Canal corridor in order to attend to personnel and equipment needs of their ships.

Suppliers do a brisk business with passing ships. Food orders from the cook, especially for perishable items, are loaded as the ship is raised or lowered in a lock. Linen and uniforms are cleaned and returned to the ship before it exits the waterway. Equipment sales and repairs occur both during the navigation season as well as during winter lay-up, providing business to area merchants.

A refuelling dock above Lock 8 at Port Colborne can send vessels on their way with a quick fill-up.

Port Weller Dry Docks above Lock 1 is a major shipbuilder, with lake and ocean-going freighters, an Arctic class bulk carrier/tanker, coastal ferries and an icebreaker to their credit. They have done major reconstruction jobs on ships and perform ship repair in the event of damage, plus routine maintenance work. They also operate a smaller drydock at Port Colborne below Lock 8.

At Thorold the Industrial Docks and Supplies Ltd. handles a variety of cargoes. Bauxite from Guyana, Trinidad, New Guinea, China and Australia is unloaded there for five area abrasives producers. Manganese and chrome ore come from Belgium, Brazil and Africa. Silica quartz, petroleum, coke and salt are also unloaded.

Across the water from the Industrial dock the Ontario Paper Company dock receives a steady supply of caustic soda for their operations.

The Welland Industrial Dock can handle many types of cargo but is not as busy as docks at Port Colborne. A number of commodities are processed at this southern terminus of the Welland canal.

Grain is both loaded and unloaded at the Government and Robin Hood Elevators in Port Colborne. In addition corn is discharged for the Canada Starch plant north of the city. Stone destined for Lake Erie ports regularly clears the Century Stone Dock in Port Colborne while coal and road salt are unloaded above Lock 8 for local use.

Fishing boats, active on Lake Erie, tie up at Port Colborne as do vessels associated with offshore drilling for natural gas.

The scrapping of obsolete lakers once took place at two Port Colborne locations, but this has ceased in recent years.

The popularity of pleasure boating continues to grow. Marinas at Port Colborne and Port Dalhousie attract area residents and tourists.

Although the section of the fourth canal north of Port Colborne through Welland to Port Robinson has been abandoned for commercial navigation, it has been opened for public enjoyment of such activities as competitive rowing. The Henley Rowing Course at Port Dalhousie, above Lock 1 of the first three canals hosts major Canadian regattas each year and was chosen as the location for the 1999 World Rowing Championships.

Plans for a hiking/bicycling path following the entire canal continue to make progress. As of 1999 the section from Lock 1 south to the Glendale Bridge has been completed and is well used by walkers and roller-bladers as well as cyclists.

Mr. Merritt's canal remains a key factor in the economy of the cities and towns bordering the waterway.

Table 1: Selected Canal Statistics

PASSAGES AND TONNAGES
THROUGH THE WELLAND CANAL FROM 1930

YEAR	PASSAGES	TONNAGE
1930	5,252	6,087,910
1935	5,091	8,950,879
1940	6,850	12,909,597
1945	6,210	12,961,435
1950	7,270	14,719,346
1955	9,334	20,893,572
1960	7,536	29,249,689
1965	8,384	53,420,179
1970	7,122	62,868,908
1975	6,041	59,849,026
1980	6,567	59,605,881
1985	3,826	41,851,760
1990	3,577	39,397,900
1995	3,295	39,375,000
1998	3,492	40,395,000

*Totals from 1980 to present are given in metric tonnes.
**Courtesy St. Lawrence Seaway Authority

Port Weller Dry Docks at Lock One, with several ships undergoing maintenance and repair. (Courtesy Port Weller Dry Docks and Wayne Farrar)

6 Preserving the Past

Welland Canals Centre, Lock 3. (Don Revell)

PRESERVING THE PAST

Organizations dedicated to preserving the history of the Welland Canal have existed for years.

The Welland Canals Foundation developed out of the 150th Anniversary Committee which worked to focus on the Welland Canal in 1979. The group remains actively involved in promoting the tourist attractions of the present waterway and has assisted in the publication of books, brochures and postcards related to the navigation season.

This group has also worked for more signs recognizing the canal, helped establish a group of guides to service tour bus groups and coordinated festivities.

Each November 29 the WCF holds the annual Merritt Day celebration recalling the first voyage of the schooner ANNIE AND JANE in 1829. The first upbound ship of the day is honoured by a special celebration to mark the occasion.

The St. Catharines Museum assists the WCF and the St. Lawrence Seaway Management Corp. in recognizing the first ship of the season to navigate the canal in a special Top Hat ceremony.

The Welland Canals Centre is presently located at Lock 3 and is made up of the St. Catharines Museum, the Ontario Lacrosse Hall of Fame, a restaurant and snack bar, a museum shop and an elevated viewing platform.

The Welland Canal Ship Society, a group of marine historians and photographers, host monthly meetings and produce a bi-monthly newsletter called The Wheelhouse.

Other groups have filled an important niche over the years, including the Welland Canals Parkway Development Board. History is also preserved at three fine area museums, two of which are close to the canal.

Port Colborne Historical and Marine Museum. This is the pilothouse from the YVON DUPRE JR.

Each year, students of all ages visit the St. Catharines Museum at Lock 3 to study the geography and history of the local area. Programs have been developed by the museum's staff to integrate with the schools' curriculum. (Don Revell)

The St. Catharines Museum has permanent displays featuring the historical significance of the four Welland Canals along with a video presentation and interactive displays. The Museum also features an integrated exhibit related to the Underground Railroad and the role played in local history by Niagara's African Canadians.

The Port Colborne Historical Museum is at 280 King Street in Port Colborne. It is located south of Lock 8 on the west side of the canal. Displays include the pilot-house of the former tug YVON DUPRE JR. Each August the museum hosts a highly successful and well attended "Canal Days". Between these two, the Welland Historical Museum, at 65 Hooker Street, is within a short drive of the canal at Welland.

SPECIAL ISSUE SHIP STAMPS

Canada Post recognized the historical significance of the Welland Canal in 1974, issuing an 8-cent commemorative stamp honouring William Hamilton Merritt, who was the driving force behind the construction of the first Welland Canal.

Ships with ties to the canal have also been featured at various times, including 10-cent commemoratives of CHICORA and ATHABASCA, as part of a 1976 series on inland vessels. The LOUIS R. DESMARAIS, still a regular trader through the canal, was part of the 45-cent technology issue in 1996.

The nation of Grenada put out a 1-cent stamp on November 3, 1976 featuring the FEDERAL PALM, a passenger and freight carrier built by Port Weller Dry Docks. Later, on April 5, 1978 Tuvalu issued a 30-cent stamp recognizing this ship under her later name as CENPAC ROUNDER.

In 1998 Canada Post recognized ships of the Canadian Navy with two 45-cent issues. One featured HMCS SHAWINIGAN which has made several goodwill voyages to the Great Lakes.

Courtesy of Canada Post